SLAUGHTER
Of
TERRIFIED BEASTS

A Biblical Basis for
the Humane Treatment of Animals

*The violence done to Lebanon shall sweep
over you, the havoc done to its beasts
shall break your own spirit. (Hab 2:17)*

By
J. R. Hyland

Viatoris Ministries
Sarasota, Florida 34277

Copyright © 1988 by J. R. Hyland

Published by
Viatoris Ministries
P.O. Box 25354
Sarasota, FL 34277

PRINTED IN THE UNITED STATES OF AMERICA
First printing 1988

Designed and produced by Robinson Book Associates

Library of Congress Cataloging in Publication Data

Hyland, J.R.
   The Slaughter of Terrified Beasts
   A Biblical Basis for the Humane Treatment of Animals

   Bibliography: p.
   ISBN 0-945703-00-7
   Library of Congress Catalog Card Number 88-50200

CONTENTS

There is no difference between the pain of man and the pain of other living beings.

Maimonides

Until he extends the circle of his compassion to all living things, man will not himself find peace.

Albert Schweitzer

'Tis cruelty that makes the world awry . . . .
When men have learned that when they harm a living thing they harm themselves, they surely will not kill, nor cause a thing that God has made to suffer pain.

The Aquarian Gospel

Cruelty to animals is as if man did not love God.

Cardinal John Henry Newman

Abbreviations used with scripture quotations:

AMP—The Amplified Bible   NEB—The New English Bible
  JB—The Jerusalem Bible   NIV—The New International
NAS—The New American   Version
     Standard

When no abbreviation is used, the King James version of the Bible is being quoted.

SALES INFORMATION

Copies of this book can be ordered from
Viatoris Ministries, P.O. Box 25354,
Sarasota, FL 34277. (Phone 813-924-8887)
Please send $8.50 to cover cost of book,
postage and handling.

PROLOGUE

PROGRESSIVE REVELATION IS a concept accepted by theologians of diverse backgrounds and loyalties. It has to do with the belief that although God's self-revelation does not change, the human capacity to receive that revelation does change. It grows and develops as people progress in their ability to understand who God is and what constitutes right relationship to the Creator.

This progressive understanding led to the repudiation of human sacrifices as well as to the progress from polytheistic to monotheistic belief. And in the time of the Latter Prophets of Israel, the concept of social justice as a measure of righteousness and conformity with the will of God came to the fore. Prophets like Isaiah, Jeremiah, Micah, and Amos told their people that the true worship of God manifested itself in the just and compassionate treatment of the helpless and powerless, not in ceremonial or sacrificial rituals. The revelation given by those prophets also concerned man's relationship to animal life. The abuse of animals—like the oppression of human beings—is opposed to the way of life that God has ordained. And although the world has fallen far short of the standards

1

given by God, the Prophetic Age signaled that it was time for the human race to remember its beginnings. It was time to try to live the kind of life that God ordained at the Creation.

Through the prophets, God called the people to "beat their swords into plowshares" (Isa. 2:4) and promised a better world if they did not "oppress the alien, the orphan or the widow." (Jer. 7:6) A world of justice and nonviolence was also a world that did not abuse animals in the name of their Creator. There was to be no more sacrifice of animals on the altars of God: "I have no pleasure in the blood of lambs and goats .... Take your evil deeds out of my sight." (Isa. 1:11, 16)

The advent of the Prophetic Age in Israel marked a milestone in the spiritual journey of the people of God. There was a breakthrough in consciousness and a call to justice, mercy, and compassion that still sounds in our own day. But today—as in biblical times—there is still an adamant refusal to follow that call. There is still a reactionary effort to make the worship of God a thing of ceremony and ritual rather than a matter of compassionate treatment for all creatures.

Human beings continue to exercise their free will in other negative ways—by waging war, perpetrating social injustice, and exploiting animal life. Too often they claim that such actions are in accord with God's plan for the earth. Consequently, these ungodly actions are carried out in the name of God.

But there are others who struggle to build a world of peace, justice, and compassion for all forms of life. They try to walk in the light that the Spirit shines into our darkness. That Spirit continually seeks to lead the human race out of the violence and selfishness that made a hell out of the paradise that God prepared for all creatures.

THE SLAUGHTER
OF TERRIFIED BEASTS

THE EIGHTH CENTURY B.C. inaugurated an era of spiritual and moral evolution in Judaism that struggles to continue in our own day. It was a giant leap in consciousness that seemed to emerge, full blown, in the teachings of the Latter Prophets.

The teachings of those men affirmed the primary importance of social justice, rejected ceremonial and sacrificial religion, and articulated a change from henotheism to monotheism. They also taught that Homo sapiens is not the end-all or be-all of God's creation—that, in fact, the animal kingdom is an integral part of the Kingdom to come. It would be a peaceable kingdom where "they shall not hurt or destroy in all my holy mountain: for the earth shall be full of the knowledge of the Lord." (Isa. 11:9)

Although this change in consciousness regarding animals was first articulated in the Hebrew scriptures, students of religion have traditionally credited India with the concept. They point to the teachings of Buddha and Mahavira, both of whom denounced the sacrifice of animals in the sixth century B.C. The Hinduism of their day required the slaughter of sacrificial animals; it was an integral part of that religion.

As is usual in a sacrificial cult, the priests wielded great power. The power of the Brahmin priests rested on the teaching that only they could offer the kind of sacrifices that were "the atonement for everything ... the sacrifice that redeems all sin." [1] Only the priests were empowered to utter the sacred formula over such sacrifices; they were the intermediaries between the gods and men. They alone could insure that the gods were propitiated and that petitions would be granted. Without their mediation the people would be lost—they would be out of favor with the forces on whom they thought their very lives depended.

Of course, the priests were not going to accept any teaching that repudiated the animal sacrifice that was the cornerstone of their power. Consequently, they saw Buddha and Mahavira as enemies. Not only did these sages teach that sacrificial worship did not secure the blessings of any god, they also taught that such sacrifices were intrinsically evil. They taught that inflicting pain and death on other sentient creatures retarded the spiritual growth of human beings. Since animals were equipped with the same five senses as human beings, taught Mahavira, they could obviously experience the same sensations of pain, suffering, and fear. To abuse these creatures in the name of any god was an affront to the concept of Deity.

---

1. Noss, John B. *Man's Religions*, 6th ed. (New York: Macmillan Publishing Co., Inc., 1980), p. 83.

Because these teachings against sacrifice could not be contained within the Hinduism of their time, they became part of the separate religions of Buddhism and Jainism. When that happened, the substance of these new teachings stood out in clear distinction from Hindu doctrine. As these new religions developed, the concept of nonviolence toward man and all other creatures was reinforced.

But India was not the setting for the first religious reaction against animal sacrifice. The understanding that the suffering and death of animals was repugnant to the Creator had surfaced among the Hebrews long before Indian sages articulated such concepts. Beginning with Isaiah in 750 B.C., the Latter Prophets condemned animal sacrifice. In so doing these prophets were reiterating the ancient knowledge found in Genesis: Animals were created in love and goodness, just as human beings had been. And humans were ordained to be the loving caretakers of animals, not their cruel abusers.

Although the Judaic prophecies regarding animals and their treatment predated the teachings in India, the message of the Latter Prophets did not stand out in clear relief because their teachings did not break from Judaism to form a separate belief system. Instead, their prophetic message was absorbed into the mainstream of the Hebrew religion and became still another current running through the spiritual history of Israel. Consequently, the warnings against sacrificial religion continued to coexist with a priestly power structure that was still developing complex rituals for slaughter.

This coexistence of opposing viewpoints is a great strength of the Old Testament; it is one of the reasons for its continuing impact on the human race. The Hebrew scriptures record both the continuity and the changes that took place in Judaism's understanding of God. They tell of the struggle between opposing values that continued for many centuries. The scriptures also provide a continuous, if selective, chronicle of a nation's spiritual journey.

The Old Testament does not gloss over the negative history of its people. The good and the bad, the going forward and the sliding back, the high points of the nation's history and its nadir—all are included in the record. But in reading this record it is important to understand that negative developments do not always receive a negative comment. Often, it is only when a later generation adds to the biblical record that it becomes evident that certain events had not received the unqualified endorsement that earlier accounts seemed to present. The story of Jacob and Esau is a case in point.

Although he cheated his brother of his birthright, the original account in the book of Genesis does not comment negatively on the fact that Jacob deliberately cheated his brother. But hundreds of years after the fact, the Bible does refer to Jacob's deception as something blameworthy. [2] This negative assessment of Jacob's action was not a new thought in Judaism; it had long been present in Israel's discussions and disputa-

---

2. Isa. 43:27; Jer. 9:4; Hosea 12:2, 3. AMP.

tions of the incident. Eventually this negative judgment of the event became part of the biblical record.

The same kind of deferred judgment occurs regarding the sacrifice of animals. For centuries the scriptures presented a seemingly one-sided view of the practice —a view that implied sacrifice was unquestioningly accepted in Israel. But during that time there was an undercurrent that opposed such worship. And with the advent of the Prophet Isaiah in the eighth century B.C., that current surfaced and entered the mainstream of Hebrew life. Opposition to the entrenched rituals of sacrificial worship then became part of the biblical record.

Because widely divergent viewpoints like these can only appear as contradictions in a short-term view of events, an overview of the Bible is necessary. An overview provides a long-term perspective. We see that it is conflict—not contradiction—that the Bible is reporting. Many ideals struggled for supremacy in Judaism over the centuries, and the various books of the Old Testament provide different perspectives on those conflicts.

Without an overview and without a knowledge of the deferred judgment that is applied to some biblical events, it would seem that suddenly, for no discernible reason, there was a reaction in Judaism against the sacrifice of animals. This sudden reaction would be doubly confusing because at the time that the prophets began speaking out against the slaughter, the cult of Temple worship was at a zenith. And the ritual slaughter of animals was at the heart of that worship.

The priests who officiated at the sacrifices had enormous religious and political power. Like their Hindu counterparts, the Israelite priests had a vested interest in sacrificial worship. They had developed complex and intricate rituals for slaughter, all with appropriate prayers to God. Those rituals had become completely integrated into their sacred tradition. By the time Isaiah began his prophetic ministry, slaughtering animals in the name of God had assumed the nature of an additional commandment in the eyes of the people.

But Isaiah, and those who followed him, called the people back from their violent worship. The Lord, they said, had never asked for the slaughter of His own creatures: It was man himself who had instituted sacrificial worship.

The prophets also sought to reestablish the teaching contained in the book of beginnings—the book of Genesis. Genesis taught that animals, like human beings, were created by God; that God had concern for their welfare, just as He had for human welfare. And as surely as the Lord had established a covenant with human creatures, so He had also covenanted with other creatures—with the beasts of the field and the birds of the air. [3]

The prophecies of men like Isaiah, Micah, and Amos reiterated that the sacrifice of animals was an abomination in the sight of God, an unholy practice that

---

3. See chapter 3, "After The Flood."

demanded repentance. Isaiah was the first of his era to prophesy against the sacrificial cult:

> The multitude of your sacrifices—what are they to me? says the Lord. I have more than enough of burnt offerings of rams and the fat of fattened animals; I have no pleasure in the blood of bulls and lambs and goats . . . . Your hands are full of blood; wash and make yourselves clean. Take your evil deeds out of my sight. (Isa. 1:11, 15, 16 NIV)

Jeremiah, Amos, and Hosea were equally vocal about the evils of animal sacrifice. They all spoke out in the name of God against the killing taking place on the altars:

> For Ephraim in his sin has multiplied altars, altars have become his sin. Though they sacrifice flesh as offerings to me and eat them, I, the Lord will not accept them. Their guilt will be remembered and their sins punished. They shall go back to Egypt . . . . (Hosea 8:13 NEB)

They would "go back to Egypt" because when they lived in captivity there, the sacrificial cult was not yet an established Hebrew tradition. The prophet knew his people had to go back in their understanding to a time when they had not been conditioned to accept animal sacrifice as a necessary part of their worship.

The prophet Jeremiah also addressed this issue of the development of sacrificial worship and pointed back to the time when the Hebrews were first freed from their captivity in Egypt:

> Thus says the Lord of hosts, the God of Israel: Add your burnt offerings to your sacrifices and eat flesh. For I did not speak to your fathers, or command them in the day

that I brought them out of the land of Egypt, concerning burnt offerings and sacrifices. But this is what I commanded them saying, 'Obey My voice and I will be your God and you will walk in all the way which I command you, that it may be well with you.' Yet they did not obey or incline their ear, but walked in their own counsels and in the stubbornness of their own heart, and went backward and not forward. Since the day that your fathers came out of the land of Egypt until this day . . . . (Jer. 7:21-25 NAS)

The Prophet Amos raised his voice in condemnation of sacrificial worship. He, too, reminded the people of the time when their ancestors left Egypt; a time when the rituals of animal sacrifice had not yet become a cornerstone of their sacred tradition. During the forty years of wandering in the wilderness they were taken care of by God—there was no need for elaborate ceremonies and festivals. Speaking in the name of the Lord, Amos forcefully declared:

I hate and despise your feasts, I take no pleasure in your solemn festivals. When you offer me holocausts, I reject your oblations, and refuse to look at your sacrifices of fattened cattle . . . but let justice flow like water, and integrity like an unfailing stream. Did you bring me sacrifice and oblation in the wilderness for all those forty years, House of Israel? (Amos 5:21, 22, 24, 25 JB)

If the chosen people were to continue their spiritual leadership, they would have to accept the prophets' message. They would have to accept that God was not pleased by a worship in which His creatures were dragged, in a frenzy, to be slaughtered in His name.

The Prophet Jeremiah voiced God's indictment of the human race as a species that took advantage of the most helpless in its midst—a race that abused those without the power to protect themselves. He juxtaposed the abuse of powerless humans with the slaughter of helpless animals on the altars of the Temple.

> Thus says the Lord of Hosts, the God of Israel: Amend your ways . . . . Do not trust in deceptive words saying, This is the temple of the Lord, the temple of the Lord, the temple of the Lord! . . . [but] if you do not oppress the alien, the orphan or the widow and do not shed innocent blood in this place, then I will let you dwell in the land that I gave to your fathers . . . . (Jer. 7:3, 4, 6, 7 NAS)

The call for the rejection of animal sacrifice was also the call for a religion marked by social justice. Ceremonies, sacrifices, and religious feast days were not pleasing to the Lord. The relief of the sufferings of the helpless and the oppressed constituted the true worship of God.

> What are your multiplied sacrifices to me? . . . . I take no pleasure in the blood of bulls, lambs or goats . . . . I hate your new moon and your appointed feasts . . . . Cease to do evil. Learn to do good; seek justice; reprove the ruthless; Defend the orphan, plead for the widows: . . . . (Isa. 1:11, 14, 16, 17 NAS)

Not only did the prophets point out that sacrifices and ceremonies were man-made substitutes for the true worship of God, they also faced their people with the fact that the violence done to sacrificial animals was reflected in the violence that human beings were willing to inflict on each other. And slaughtering animals, as an act of worship among the Hebrews, was eventually reflected in the practice of human sacrifice.

Although Judaism never condoned human sacrifice, by the time of the Latter Prophets the sacrifice even of their own children had become widespread among the people. Some of those who believed that God was pleased by the slaughter of animals eventually concluded that He would be even more pleased by the sacrifice of human flesh—the flesh of their own children.

In the Book of Micah, that prophet made the connection between the sacrifice of human flesh and the sacrifice of animals.

> With what shall I come before the Lord . . . . Shall I come to Him with burnt offerings, with yearling calves? Does the Lord take delight in thousands of rams, in ten thousand rivers of oil: *Shall I present my firstborn for my rebellious acts, the fruit of my body for the sin of my soul?* [4] He has told you, O man what is good . . . do justice, to love kindness, and to walk humbly with your God. (Micah 6:6-8 NIV)

In their oracles, the Latter Prophets frequently connected man's violence toward animals with the violence he directed toward other people. Just as frequently, they linked a world of peace and prosperity with a world where animals, as well as human beings, would be free from exploitation.

A peaceable world was necessarily a world in which no creature would destroy or be destroyed. It was a world where all could live their lives in security and safety. The eleventh chapter of Isaiah describes this peaceable kingdom as a time and place wherein the

---

4. Italics used for emphasis are mine throughout.

human race will strive to live in accord with the Divinity in whose image it was created. And in that kind of world, the animal kingdom will reflect the goodness and mercy that will be the hallmark of human affairs.

> . . . with righteousness He will judge the needy, with justice He will give decisions for the poor of the earth . . . . The wolf will live with the lamb, the leopard will lie down with the goat and the calf and the lion and the yearling together: and a little child will lead them. (Isa. 11:4, 6 NIV)

The prophet went on to further describe this peace that will be evident among the animals as well as among men.

> The cow and the bear make friends, their young lie down together. The lion eats straw like the ox. The infant plays over the cobras hole; into the vipers lair the young child puts his hand. They do not hurt, nor harm, on all my holy mountain, for the country is filled with the knowledge of the Lord as the waters swell the sea. (Isa. 11:7-9 JB)

This knowledge that fills the world "as the waters swell the sea" is the knowledge of a rule of justice and compassion. It is a rule that people will finally accept; a rule that rejects the unjust and violent behavior that human beings demonstrated so often.

Like Isaiah, the Prophet Micah spoke of a time when people will be willing to put into practice what they learn—a time when they will act in a way that conforms to the way God would have things done:

> Come and let us go to the mountain of the Lord and to the house of the God of Jacob, that He may teach us about His

ways . . . . Then they will hammer their swords into plowshares and their spears into pruning hooks; Nation will not lift up sword against nation. And never again will they train for war. And each of them will sit under his vine and under his fruit tree with no one to make them afraid. (Micah 4:2, 3, 4, NAS)

Still another of the prophets—Hosea—prophesied that there would be no more war. There would be no war because human behavior would be marked by love and compassion. It would be a time when men would renounce their violence because they had had enough of the misery and suffering they had created. And in a world marked by love and compassion, human beings would not only live in peace with each other, they would also live in peace with the beasts of the fields and the birds of the air.

In that day I will make a covenant for them with the beasts of the field and the birds of the air and the creatures that move along the ground. Bow and sword and battle I will abolish from the land so that all may lie down in safety. I will betroth you to me forever; I will betroth you in righteousness and justice, in love and compassion. (Hosea 2:18–20 NIV)

The prophets taught that God's blessings would abound only in a world where human beings rejected violence and "no longer taught war." But the journey toward that peaceable kingdom demanded that the sacrifice of animals stop. A people who remained insensitive to the travesty of a worship that called for the terrorizing and slaughter of other creatures was a people whose spiritual development was being retarded; a people who had not yet taken their first step toward a millenial world.

Amazingly, though the Latter Prophets called for the reform or abolition of many of the institutions and practices that had been sanctified by the Hebrews, their message survived in the scriptures of their people. Their words were preserved because they spoke to Judaism's deepest roots. These men of God had not introduced new concepts into Israel; they had *reintroduced* themes that went back to the very beginning—back to the time of Genesis. And their great age of prophecy was a sign that it was time for the human race to recover its spiritual heritage. Speaking in the name of God, the prophets let the people know that it was time for the world to once again reflect the qualities that God had ordained at the Creation—love, compassion, and mercy for all creatures.

IN THE BEGINNING

THE VISION of the Latter Prophets—of a time when the lion will lie down with the lamb and all earth's creatures will live in peace with each other—seems an impossible dream. It seems impossible because human beings have chosen to believe that animals and men are violent by nature. Since this is held to be a self-evident truth, any information that casts doubt on its credibility is rejected. So the creed remains intact; having evolved from animals, man's worst behavior simply confirms the fact that he has not yet outgrown his beastiality.

This view of a world in the process of evolving from barbarism to civilization can be a comforting one. No matter how badly people or societies may behave, they have come a long way from their primitive beginnings. Patience must be exhibited with Homo sapiens: Evolving from beastiality is no easy task.

The dogma is different for animals. It is generally believed that they were biologically doomed to violence, that their genes are somehow permanently programmed for killing. This belief system conveniently overlooks the facts of conditioning and adaptation. It dismisses the possibility that having become conditioned to violence, some species eventually adapted to such behavior.

The biblical view of natural history contradicts the theory that men have evolved over long periods of time to their present, higher, development. In fact, the Bible tells a story of regression, not progression.

The book of Genesis reports that both men and beasts were created with a nonviolent nature, that goodness was their innate characteristic. Genesis tells the story of creatures whose natural condition is one of peaceful coexistence with their own species and with all other species. And although all have fallen from a higher state, their innate goodness—their nonviolent nature—remains waiting to be reactivated.

Even though they have adapted to a violent lifestyle, both animals and humans can readapt to their original, peaceful natures. It is on this foundational truth that the millenial vision of the Latter Prophets was based. It was this truth that undergirded their vision of a time when, once again, humans and nonhumans would live together peaceably, in a peaceable world. It would be a world free from the fear and suffering that earth's creatures have unleashed upon themselves.

Like the prophets who linked the fate of men and animals in a millenial future, the book of Genesis links them in their far-distant past. Both humans and animals were created as extensions of God's love and goodness. All creatures had within them the same "breath of life." (Gen. 2:3) All were given the same instructions to "be fruitful and increase in number." In this picture of paradise, the man and woman were loving and trusted caregivers for the creatures among whom they lived. Theirs was a relationship of trust and leadership—not of dominance or exploitation.

The nonviolent nature of all earth's inhabitants is further delineated in the biblical report of God's plan for the sustenance of all creatures. Food was provided only from the bounty of the earth; no creature was to feed on another:

> Then God said [to the man and the woman] I give you every seed-bearing plant on the face of the whole earth and every tree that has fruit with seed in it. They will be for your food. And to all the beasts of the earth and all the birds in the air and all the creatures that move on the ground—everything that has breath of life in it—I give every green plant for food. And it was so. God saw all that He had made and it was very good." (Gen. 1:28-31 NIV)

There is no information regarding the amount of time it took for this idyllic existence to end, but the third chapter of Genesis reports a degeneration that has already taken place. The man and woman have chosen to partake of evil; they have chosen to "know" good *and* evil (Gen. 3:22), where before they had "known" only the good.

Once they had chosen to know evil, the degeneration of Adam and Eve reached the point where they were no longer able to respect or abide by the rules of a paradisiacal existence. Consequently, they had to leave Eden. Their new environment reflected their regressive behavior.

Because humans were their leaders, the animals reflected their fall from a higher estate. In our age of ecological concern it is easier to understand how the negative behavior of human beings adversely affected the life around them. It reached the point that the very earth was "cursed."

> Cursed is the ground because of you . . . it will produce thorns and thistles for you and you will eat the plants of the fields by the sweat of your brow. (Gen. 3:17, 18, 19 NIV)

No longer would the lush bounty of earth automatically provide Adam and Eve with nourishment, and the animals would share the human fate of having to labor and forage for their food. Together all had enjoyed an Edenic existence; together they had deteriorated from their high estate. The Book of Genesis records that together they continued to deteriorate until, at last, the earth could no longer support the violence of its inhabitants. "The earth was corrupt in God's sight and full of violence." (Gen. 6:11)

> The Lord saw how great man's wickedness on the earth had become, and every inclination of the thoughts of his heart was only evil, all the time . . . . So the Lord said: I will wipe mankind, whom I have created, from the face of the earth—man and animals and creatures that move along the ground and birds of the air—for I am grieved that I have made them. (Gen. 6:5, 7 NIV)

The waters of a great Flood would wash away this uncivilized civilization. But a remnant would survive. The Lord spoke to Noah; he and his family would be saved from the coming catastrophe—however, there was a condition to be fulfilled: If man were to survive he had to fulfill his role of caregiver for the animals.

Nonhumans as well as human beings had to be provided with safe passage.

Noah's commission to provide for the animals is a story of crucial importance. The Bible has already told how God gave man responsibility for the care and welfare of other creatures at the time of Creation; how, by the time of the Flood, he had already corrupted himself and abused that responsibility. Nevertheless, the scripture makes it clear that accountability for the animals would continue to be a fact of human existence. Without safe passage for them, there would be no safe passage for Noah and his family.

It took a prodigious amount of time and work for Noah to construct something large enough to contain all the creatures who were to survive the Flood. It took an enormous effort for man to fulfill his responsibility as caregiver for the other creatures of earth. But if he were to survive as a species, he had to fulfill his caregiver role.

The animals who survived—like Noah and his family—were individually called to be saved from the Flood. God communicated His message to specific animals and, two by two, they presented themselves to Noah:

> And Noah and his sons and his wife and his sons' wives entered the ark to escape the waters of the flood. Pairs of clean and unclean animals, and of all creatures ... *came to Noah*[4] and entered the ark. (Gen. 7:8 NIV)

> Pairs of all creatures that have the breath of life in them *came to Noah* and entered the Ark. (Gen. 7:15 NIV)

AFTER THE FLOOD

> God remembered Noah and the wild animals and the
> livestock that were with him in the ark and He sent a wind
> over the earth and the waters receded. (Gen. 8:1 NIV)

"GOD REMEMBERED NOAH and the wild animals." The
biblical record of post-Flood events begins with this
continued revelation of God's equal concern for human
and nonhuman creatures. This theme is repeated in
the story of the descent from the ark.

> Then God said to Noah, come out of the ark, you and your
> wife and your sons and their wives. Bring out every kind
> of living creature that is with you—the birds, the animals
> and all the creatures that move along the ground—so they
> can multiply on the earth and be fruitful and increase in
> number on it. (Gen. 8:15, 16, 17 NIV)

> God blessed Noah and his sons, saying to them, Be fruitful
> and fill the earth. (Gen. 9:1 NIV)

Both animals and men are commanded, "be fruitful
and multiply." As in the creation account birds, beasts,
and human beings are given the same instructions.
(Gen. 1:22, 28) This theme of equal treatment and equal
concern is given an ultimate reinforcement in the story
of the covenant that God made with earth's inhabitants

after the Flood. In fact, the biblical passage that tells of this covenant is unique—it gives the same message five times in one paragraph. (Gen. 9:8–17)

In the Hebrew scriptures, repetition is used to signal that what is being said is extremely important. In this case, the critical message repeated the fact that God was entering into a covenant relationship with animals as well as with men.

(1) This is the sign of the covenant I am making between Me and you and every living creature . . . a covenant for all generations to come. I have set My rainbow in the clouds and it will be the sign of the covenant. (Gen. 9:11, 13 NIV)

(2) Then God said to Noah . . . I now establish My covenant with you and your descendants after you and with every living creature that was with you—the birds, the livestock and all the wild animals, all those that came out of the ark with you—every living creature on earth. (Gen. 9:8–10 NIV)

(3) Whenever I bring clouds over the earth and the rainbow appears in the clouds I will see it and I will remember My covenant between Me and you and all living creatures of every kind. (Gen. 9:14–15 NIV)

(4) Whenever the rainbow appears in the clouds I will see it and remember the everlasting covenant between God and all living creatures of every kind on the earth. (Gen. 9:16 NIV)

(5) So God said to Noah, this is the sign of the covenant I have established between Me and all life on earth. (Gen. 9:17 NIV)

The idea of covenanting with God is an exalted concept—a sacred phenomenon. In biblical terms it constitutes a unique relationship—a special bonding. And the constant repetition that God made this special bond between Himself and the animals came at a crucial point in the history of the earth. Just as life after the Fall in Eden was life lived at a much regressed level, so life after the Flood was a much lower order of existence than it had been before.

The world that was washed away by the waters of the Flood was a world that had nurtured and influenced all those who survived in the ark; and it was a heritage of corruption and degeneracy. The extent of that decay is most vividly presented by the Amplified Bible, as it describes the world in which Noah and the other survivors had lived.

> The earth was depraved and putrid in God's sight and the land was filled with violence (desecration, infringement, outrage, assault, and lust for power). And God looked upon the world and saw how degenerate, debased and vicious it was, for all humanity had corrupted their way upon the earth and lost their true direction. (Gen. 6:11-12)

This was the kind of world that had nurtured Noah and his family. And this was the world in which Noah was outstanding for his righteousness. The Bible tells why he was saved from the flood.

> Noah found favor in the eyes of the Lord. This is the account of Noah. *Noah was a righteous man, blameless among the people of his time.* (Gen. 6:8, 9 NIV)

The generation in which Noah was declared a "righteous man" was the same generation in which "all humanity" had lost their way—"their true direction." And as the story of Noah's actions after the Flood makes clear, he did not escape the world's debasing influence. (Gen. 9:21) It is a testimony to the goodness and mercy of God, not to the goodness of Noah, that he was saved from the waters of the Flood. Noah's effort to follow a higher standard of behavior than his neighbors was counted for "righteousness" and was rewarded by God. But that higher standard was relative.

The idea of being *relatively* righteous—of being the best in a situation where the best is none too good—is repeated elsewhere in the scriptures. In an incident that takes place many generations after Noah's time, God tells the Hebrew people it is not because of their righteousness that they are being allowed to enter the promised land of Canaan.

> It is not because of your righteousness or your integrity that you are going in to take possession of their land; but on account of the wickedness of those nations. (Deut. 9:5)

The above-quoted scripture was given after the forty years of wandering in the wilderness. But God's preservation of them during that time was no reason for the Israelites to be lulled into a false sense of security. Like Noah, those who survived in the wilderness were good only relative to the wickedness of other people. Noah's behavior was acceptable only in comparison with the utterly depraved behavior of his neighbors.

The man whom God saved from the forty days of

rain was the survivor of a human race that had so corrupted itself that it could no longer live up to its former standards of behavior. The violence to which the creatures of earth had conditioned themselves had caused their regression. The results of that regression are detailed in Genesis 6:11-12. And these details give the reason for the repetitiveness of the covenant story. They reveal why the scriptures keep emphasizing that God cared so much for the animals that he entered into the same covenant relationship with them as He did with men. It was necessary to repeat that information so many times because men had regressed to the point where they would abuse animals and use them in unnatural ways. This nadir of human development is spelled out in the Bible. God tells Noah and his sons:

> The fear and dread of you will fall upon all the beasts of the earth and all the birds of the air, upon every creature that moves along the ground and upon all the fish of the sea. Everything that lives and moves will be food for you. Just as I gave you the green plant, I now give you everything. (Gen. 9:2, 3 NIV)

Human chauvinism has prompted some exegetes to see this passage of scripture as constituting God's blessing on man-turned-carnivore. But the passage does not signify divine approval of what has taken place. It is not approval—it is acceptance of what has already happened. Just as the Lord accepted that Adam and Eve chose to "know" evil and consequently were unsuited for life in Eden, He now accepted that man—and other creatures—had regressed to feeding on each other's flesh. And although the Bible does not tell us at what point various species made this adaptation, it had taken place by the time of the Flood, when the world had become "degenerate, debased, and vicious."

By Noah's day, many of earth's creatures had changed from herbiverous to carnivorous organisms— even though God had created all His creatures to be nurtured only by the produce of the earth:

> Everything that has the breath of life in it ... I give every green plant for food. (Gen. 1:30)

The restriction to plant sources as the only legitimate form of food was the standard to which all of earth's creatures had been held from the beginning of time. But during the millenia that had passed since then, man had become conditioned—and adapted—to a much lower form of life. Noah and his family, like the people among whom they lived, had become carnivorous. And human development had reached such a nadir that the survivors of the flood could no longer be held to former standards of behavior. Thus God's mercy kept pace with man's regression.

Human understanding had darkened to the point where it could no longer comprehend the higher level on which it had once lived. There were still some food restrictions, however, that human beings had to observe:

> You must not eat meat that has its lifeblood still in it. (Gen. 9:3)

This verse of scripture has given rise to many religious regulations that developed around the slaughter of animals. Whether or not an animal's body still had blood in it became a matter of ritual cleanliness. But the point of the scripture is not a concern with whether or not the carcass had blood in it. The meaning is much more primitive and direct: Human beings were being forbidden to eat creatures that were still alive.

In a regressed world, some animal species were allowed even that. But for human beings this was an ultimate taboo. Unlike animals who devoured their still-struggling prey, man had to be sure that what he ate was dead. Other translations of the Bible make the point clearly:

> You must not eat flesh with life . . . JB

> Only you shall not eat flesh with its life . . . NAS

> But you must not eat the flesh with the life . . . NEB

The fact that ancient peoples equated life with blood was a safeguard against a gradual slackening of this food taboo. The blood/life belief spawned religious rituals that insured no blood was left in meat that was to be consumed. Draining the blood insured that the animal was dead. Without this safeguard, the taboo against eating living flesh probably would have eroded over a period of time, and human beings would have devolved even further.

Homo sapiens was not a species that simply continued on after the Flood. Human beings had gone far backward in the framework of time and space. Instead of the balance of nature that had originally provided food for all creatures from the bounty of the earth, there was now a debased system in which every creature could be the prey of another. And the scriptural prophecy that "the fear and dread" of man would fall on the animals also became true for other human beings. Man would prey upon man; the powerful would consume the lives and substance of the less powerful—man or beast.

ABRAHAM AND BEYOND

Part I: The Patriarch

AFTER THE TIME OF NOAH there was a long period during which there is no biblical report of God's special dealings with an individual. That hiatus begins in prehistorical times and does not end until circa 2,000 B.C. The long silence ends with the story of Sarah and Abraham, founding parents of Judaism. The biblical account of their lives and loves gives many clues regarding the kind of human development that had been taking place since the time of the Flood.

The information given indicates that man's understanding had remained darkened and that his violence had continued unabated. Abraham's attempt to sacrifice his son Isaac shows this trend clearly. In Abraham's day, human sacrifice had become an acceptable way of worshipping God. Because it was acceptable, the patriarch could set out to Moriah fully expecting to murder his son there.

Because theologians have so admired Abraham's obedience in trying to carry out the sacrifice he thought God was demanding, they have ignored a critical issue in the story. This account of Isaac's near-death is pointing out that at its very inception, Judaism chose a higher path than contemporary religions: It substituted animal sacrifice for human sacrifice.

> When they reached the place God had told him about, Abraham built an altar there . . . . He bound his son Isaac and laid him on the altar, on top of the wood. Then he reached out his hand and took the knife to slay his son. But the angel of the Lord called out to him . . . . Do not lay a hand on the Boy . . . . Abraham looked up and there in a thicket he saw a ram. . . . He went over and took the ram and sacrificed it as a burnt offering. (Gen. 22:9–13 NAS)

A substitute for Isaac—a ram—was provided at the last minute. This was not done to satisfy God's need *for* sacrifice. It was done because of Abraham's need *to* sacrifice. The patriarch had gone to Moriah to worship in this way; he would not leave without doing so. To him, such an omission would have represented the worst kind of sacrilege. At this point of human regression, Abraham was incapable of understanding that the sacrifice of any flesh—human or nonhuman—was an abomination to God. It would be many hundreds of years before that message could be communicated by the Latter Prophets. The human race had fallen so far in its development that it could only begin climbing to its former state a step at a time. In Abraham's day, the crucial first step was the renunciation of human sacrifice. The next step—the rejection of animal sacrifice—would have to come later.

When Abraham took that crucial step of rejecting human sacrifice, he assured his descendants a pivotal place in God's unfolding plan. Without that rejection, the patriarch and his descendants could not have been the people chosen to represent the spiritual evolution of the human race. Abraham was able to substitute a ram for his son. After that incident it was always understood that the God of Abraham was a God who rejected human sacrifice. Though there would be many times when some of the Israelites would imitate their less-developed neighbors and offer their own children on sacrificial altars, Judaism never required such a sacrifice; it was always understood that human sacrifices were an "abomination" to the God of Israel. But not until the advent of the Latter Prophets did the people begin to accept that the sacrifice of animals was also repugnant in God's sight.

Over a thousand years elapsed between Abraham's rejection of human sacrifice and Isaiah's prophecies against animal sacrifice. During that time, the human race continued its worship of violence and the biblical record of those years presents a near-constant account of human and animal slaughter. But there is a brief respite: The Bible tells of an attempt to condition an entire people to a life that was not violent to either men or animals. This attempt took place when the Hebrew people wandered for forty years in the wilderness of the Sinai Peninsula.

Part II: The Wilderness

The children of Israel walked forty years in the wilderness
till all the people that were men of war, which came out of
Egypt, were consumed. (Josh. 5:6 JB)

Under the leadership of Moses, the Hebrew people
were freed from the yoke of Egyptian bondage.
Although once prosperous in Egypt, a time came when
they lost all privileges and power and were reduced to
the status of slaves. Finally, in the midst of their
suffering and deprivation, Moses came to lead them
out of Pharaoh's land and begin the journey to Canaan.

The Bible describes Canaan—the Promised Land—
as a place "flowing with milk and honey." The image is
pastoral and nonviolent. This word-picture of a bountiful land is an attempt to awaken the memory of a
paradise now lost. Only in a land where the inhabitants
do not prey on each other could there be the kind of
peaceful cooperation between men and other creatures
that would yield such abundance that it would seem to
be "flowing with milk and honey."

This image of bountiful nourishment that did not
necessitate the slaughter of any creature was presented
to a people accustomed to eating flesh—a people who
equated the eating of meat with being well fed. Only a
few months after they were freed from Egyptian
slavery, one of the people's chief complaints was that
they missed the "flesh pots" of Egypt. Specifically,
they bemoaned the lack of meat—something they had

enjoyed even as slaves. In fact, their desire for this kind of food became so strong that the Hebrews declared they were better off in Egypt because there, at least, they were given flesh to eat. (Nu. 11:18)

In the first months of their wilderness journey, when the conditioning to such food was still strong among the people, they had been provided with the meat they demanded. (Ex. 16:12) But later, when they had been weaned from such a diet by years of eating the manna that God provided, such demands were not acceptable. (Nu. 11:4–34)

The years of being sustained in the desert by manna were also years during which all the "men of war" perished. The violence of war and the violence of animal slaughter were in abeyance for most of the wilderness years. But the experiment in nonviolent living failed. When the forty years were over and the Hebrews were ready to enter the Promised Land, the people once again began eating flesh, and the manna no longer fell from heaven.

The Bible gives an account of the way in which the Israelites entered Jericho. No weapons of war were used to penetrate the walls of that Canaanite city. Instead, the sons of Israel marched around the city in a prescribed ritual for seven days. Then the trumpets were sounded, the people shouted, and the walls collapsed. (Josh. 6:20) It was a unique method of entry for a people among whom all the "men of war" had died. No one was killed in the attempt to breach the walls; but after the city fell, the time of nonviolence was over. The Israelites entered the town and proceeded to slaughter all the inhabitants as easily as any seasoned warriors could have done: "They destroyed with the sword every living thing in it—men and women, young and old, cattle, sheep and donkey." (Josh. 6:21)

Once again human beings and animals suffered the same fate: All were slaughtered in the takeover. And the Bible records that man's violence in the land continued unabated—and undenounced—for more than 500 years. During those centuries neither priest nor prophet raised a voice to protest either the human or the animal slaughter that was carried out in the name of the Lord. Instead, the priests taught that such slaughter glorified God.

But eventually the Latter Prophets intruded on this santification of violence. It was Jeremiah who denounced the massacre that had taken place when the Hebrews entered Jericho. Speaking in the name of God he told the people that the wholesale slaughter that had taken place when their ancestors entered Canaan had been an abomination in the sight of God—not something to be celebrated.

> I brought you into a fruitful land to enjoy its fruit and the goodness of it, but when you entered upon it you defiled it and made the home I gave you loathsome. (Jer. 2:5-7 JB)

Denunciations like this had not been heard in Israel. To the contrary, violence in the name of God had become an integral part of religious practices. The victories that resulted in the slaughter of human enemies were celebrated with the slaughter of animals; their blood was endlessly poured over Jahweh's altars as thanksgiving for past triumphs or inducements for future victories. Such mayhem was always accompanied by prayers and petitions. Numerous blessings and rituals were developed to sanctify the slaughters that took place on the altars of war as well as on the altars of the Temple.

Ultimately, the sacrificial and ceremonial aspects of religious worship became so firmly entrenched in Judaism that those rituals became totally identified with the worship of God. This was the false worship— the false religion—from which the Latter Prophets called the people to repent. Their insistence that ceremony and sacrifice give way to social justice and nonviolence characterized the epoch of the great prophets of Israel.

For two hundred years their prophetic warnings were heard. But during those centuries there were periods of great prosperity for Judaism; although the people were warned that their violence and selfishness were sowing the seeds of destruction in their own land, a prosperous and powerful nation saw no reason to change. The Temple remained the center of sacrifice, while the poor continued to be exploited by the wealthy.

Then, history intervened.

POSTEXILIC JUDAISM

IN 587 B.C. JERUSALEM FELL to the Babylonian army. The Temple was destroyed and the Jewish people were exiled to the Land of their conquerors. The Babylonian exile lasted fifty years. During those years no animals could be slaughtered on the Temple altars, so instead of sacrificial worship, the people began to form synagogues. There, they and their descendants would gather together in the name of the Lord for thousands of years to come.

Eventually, the Babylonians themselves were defeated by the Persians. It was a propitious victory as far as the Hebrews were concerned. Cyrus, king of Persia, was very favorably disposed toward the Jews, and he allowed those who so desired to return to Jerusalem. One of the first things the returnees did was to reinstate sacrificial worship.

Under the supervision of the priests and other leaders, the people built altars and once again slaughtered animals to please God. The prophets who had denounced the cult of sacrifice were all dead, but the priests were alive and well. They told the people that if they did not offer sacrifices, God would not give His blessing nor withhold His wrath. The book of Ezra records the success of the priesthood in reestablishing the cult of Temple sacrifice.

> When the seventh month came and the Israelites had settled in their towns, the people assembled as one man in Jerusalem. Then Jeshua, son of Jozadak and his fellow priests . . . began to build the altar of the God of Israel to sacrifice burnt offerings on it, in accordance with what is written in the Law of Moses, the man of God . . . they built the altar on its foundations and sacrificed burnt offerings on it to the Lord, both the morning and evening sacrifices.
> . . . After that they presented the regular burnt offerings, the New Moon sacrifices and the sacrifices for all the appointed sacred feasts of the Lord. (Ezra 3:1, 2, 3, 5 NIV)

In resuming sacrifice, the Jewish people had reached a milestone on their spiritual journey. This choice had enormous repercussions on their subsequent history. The centrality of Temple worship gave the priests enormous power. By the fourth century B.C., the high priest—like a medieval Pope—combined the power of his religious office with the power of a secular prince.

In the centuries that followed, the sacrificial cult flourished. But the prophets had warned of the link between the violence of slaying animals on the altars of God and the violence of slaying human beings in war. Their prophecies proved true. For 500 years the Jewish people slaughtered, or were themselves slaughtered, in the endless power struggles that centered on Palestine. The blood of sacrificial victims ran deep in the House of God while the blood of war victims ran deep in the streets beyond the Temple walls.

During that period various empires ruled the land.

Persian, Macedonian, Ptolemaic, Selucid, Jewish, and Roman rulers quickly succeeded each other. Alliances with various powers were made and broken. Finally the Jewish people became embroiled in a brutal civil war in which Pharisee and Saducee tortured and killed each other as mercilessly as any outsider would have done. [1]

Although the Pharisees and Saducees were often on a murderous collision course, their fratricidal slayings of each other did not undermine the power of Temple worship. Ritual slaughter and ceremonial offerings continued unabated. Their continuance was guaranteed by a decision reached by the religious leadership. Henceforth, no individual who claimed to speak in the name of God was to be accepted as God's spokesman. By 200 B.C. it was official: The Age of Prophecy was over. The word of the Lord would now be disseminated only through established religious channels.

The postprophetic age had begun. No longer would the voices of men like Isaiah and Jeremiah be raised in protest against their own priests and political leaders. The words of those great men, now long dead, were safely enshrined in the scriptures. There they were revered, studied—and ignored.

But in spite of the fact that the Age of Prophecy had been declared dead two hundred years earlier, the voice of John the Baptist began to be heard in the wilderness of Judea. The people flocked to hear his

---

1. Josephus, Flavius, *Wars of the Jews* (Grand Rapids: Kregel Publications, 1978), 1.4.1–6.

message. John saw himself in the tradition of the Latter Prophets; he identified himself and his ministry by quoting Isaiah 40:3.

> I am as Isaiah prophesied: A voice that cries in the wilderness, make straight a way for the Lord. (John 1:23)

John's message to his people was, "Repent, for the Kingdom of Heaven is near." (Matt. 3:2) Though he was the son of a priest of Israel, the Baptist warned that claims of a specific religious heritage or belief were of no avail in the sight of God; the Lord demanded something other than traditional claims and traditional forms of worship. And when the powerful and pious Saducees and Pharisees came to investigate this prophet whose fame was spreading all over Palestine, John addressed them as "you brood of vipers." (Matt. 3.2) He continued to remain unimpressed by the religious leaders of his day.

Like the prophets who preceded him, John warned his generation that their religious observances were not pleasing to God. Their heritage of Judaism, he told the people, did not guarantee their righteousness; being a descendant of the patriarch Abraham was not a guarantee of God's favor. "Produce fruit in keeping with repentance," John told the people, "and do not begin to say to yourselves, 'We have Abraham for our father.'" (Luke 3:8)

John's popularity became so great that the people thought he might be the annointed one—the Messiah who would lead them into a victorious new era. But the Baptist rejected that idea. Instead, he witnessed to another man—to someone else who would come and reveal what God desired of his people. The one to whom John gave witness was his cousin, Jesus of Nazareth.

JESUS, THE CHRIST

JESUS DID NOT DERIVE his support from the religious leaders of his day. He never moved in the cliques of power and intrigue that surrounded the priesthood and he was always unpopular within the circles of self-regard that surrounded the pious Pharisees. Neither did the family into which he was born confer any power or prestige. His mother, Mary, was a Jewish girl of modest origins and Joseph, her husband, was a carpenter who plied his trade in the hill country of Galilee, at Nazareth.

But Jesus was not born at Nazareth. When the time for her delivery was at hand, Mary was far south, in the city of Bethlehem. Those who later became disciples of Christ understood his birthplace to be a fulfillment of the prophesy of Micah 5:2:

> ... you Bethlehem, out of you will come for men one who will be ruler over Israel, whose origins are from of old, from ancient times. (Matt. 2:6)

This prophecy was quoted in the New Testament, in the gospel of Matthew, because those who followed Christ understood that, like the prophets who had spoken before him, Jesus would teach truths from "of old, from ancient times." They were the truths that echoed the creation account of Genesis. Even the birth of Christ was a restatement of the creation story. In the biblical account, the animals were created first; man was later set in their midst as caregiver. And the story of the birth of Jesus tells how the infant was born into a place that had first sheltered and nurtured animals.

> The time came for the baby to be born. . . . She wrapped him in cloths and placed him in a manger because there was no room for them in the inn. (Luke 2:6, 7)

This theme of human/animal relatedness continues on in the Nativity story. Luke's gospel tells how the Angel of the Lord announced the birth of Christ to men who were out in the fields, caring for their animals.

> And there were shepherds living out in the fields nearby, keeping watch over their flocks at night. An angel of the Lord appeared to them . . . . 'Do not be afraid . . . I bring you good news . . . . This will be a sign to you; you will find a baby wrapped in cloths and lying in a manager. (Luke 2:8, 9, 10, 12 NIV)

So it was that those chosen to be first to know the good news of Christ's coming were men who cared for animals. They were the nurturing caregivers that God had meant man to be when Adam was placed in Eden. These shepherds were living in a way that, in their time, most closely approximated the peaceful accord between animals and men that God had ordained and the prophets had described in their millenial visions.

The work of the shepherds who attended Jesus at his

birth was the antithesis of those whose work centered around the holocaust of animals on the altars at Jerusalem. And Jesus, who was welcomed into the world by men who protected and cared for animals, never participated in the sacrificial rites of the Temple. Neither did his disciples. Just as the beginning of Judaism was marked by the rejection of human sacrifice, so the beginning of Christianity was marked by the rejection of animal sacrifice. It was a fulfillment of the call for reform that had been given by the prophets hundreds of years earlier.

But in spite of the fact that the rejection of animal sacrifice was a critical step forward in the spiritual evolution of the human race, the original followers of Jesus paid little attention to his crucial role in this development. His disciples were more concerned with his appearance as the annointed one—the Christ. In some instances, however, they did record the Master's quotation of the prophet Hosea: "I will have mercy, not sacrifice; knowledge of God, not holocausts." (Hosea 6:6) The gospel of Matthew reports two occasions on which Jesus reminded the people that Hosea had called for an end to sacrificial worship—a call that was still being ignored.[1] But it is the gospel of John that deals at greater length with the matter of Temple sacrifice.

In the fourth chapter of John's gospel there is the report of an incident that took place when Christ was in Samaria. Although of Jewish descent, the Samaritans

---

1. Matt. 9:13; 12:7.

had long intermarried with other groups, and for many centuries the full-blooded Jewish people had looked down on them. They did not consider the Samaritans to be numbered among the Chosen People. Consequently, the Samaritans had built a temple of their own, at Mt. Gerizim, where they worshipped the God of Israel. They had offered sacrifices and holocausts there until a bloody battle in 128 B.C., during which the Hebrews destroyed the rival temple.

A hundred years after that destruction, John reports that Jesus stood talking to a woman of Samaria. She pointed out that her ancestors had offered sacrifices at their own temple, but that the Jewish people never accepted those sacrifices as legitimate worship: They claimed that God only accepted the sacrifices made at the Jerusalem Temple.

"Sir," the woman said to Jesus, "I can see that you are a prophet. Our fathers worshipped on this mountain, but you Jews claim the place where we must worship is in Jerusalem." It was not an idle comment. The claim to a legitimate site for sacrificial worship was not just a matter for debate; the blood of many Samaritans and Jews had been shed over the issue. But challenged by the woman regarding the proper place for such worship, Jesus told her there was no legitimate place to offer animal sacrifices; that such worship was, in itself, antithetical to the worship of God.

> Believe me woman, a time is coming when you will worship the Father neither on this mountain nor in Jerusalem. You Samaritans worship what you do not know; we worship what we do know, for salvation is from

the Jews. Yet a time is coming and has now come when the
true worshippers will worship the Father in spirit and
truth, for they are the kind of worshippers the Father
seeks. God is spirit and his worshippers must worship in
spirit and in truth. (John 4:21-24 NIV)

In his declaration, "salvation is from the Jews," Jesus
was referring to the continuity of revelation among the
Jewish people; a continuing record of their spiritual
journey that was preserved in their scriptures. It was a
record that showed the Spirit of God repeatedly trying
to lead the human race back into the light of understanding that it had possessed at the Creation. It was
also a record of the human refusal to walk in that light.

In his declaration to the Samaritan woman, Jesus
was also prophesying the imminent destruction of the
Temple where animal sacrifices took place. For many
centuries the Jewish people had ignored prophetic
warnings to end their sacrificial worship. Now, the cult
was about to end. In A.D. 70, fewer than forty years
after Jesus announced its ruin, the Temple at Jerusalem
was destroyed. Since it was the only place where
victims could be offered to God, its destruction sig-
nalled the end of sacrificial worship in Judaism. And
from that time to this, no animals have been slaughtered on the altars of the God of Israel. But up to the
time that the Temple was destroyed, the cult of
sacrifice continued to thrive.

In predicting an end to this bloody worship, Jesus
was continuing the revelation of the Latter Prophets:
God was a loving parent who cared for all creation—
human and nonhuman. Even that which seemed of

little worth in human eyes was of value in the sight of God:

> Are not five sparrows sold for two pennies? And [yet] not one of them is forgotten or uncared for in the presence of God. (Luke 12:6 AMP)

Jesus continually revealed a God of compassion whose concern extended to all creatures. And it was the slaughter of animals, in the name of God, that led him to the only aggressive confrontation reported of his ministry. That confrontation took place at the Jerusalem Temple where Christ took direct action against the evils of sacrifice. He freed those animals who were about to be slaughtered and disrupted the entire procedure that surrounded the sacrificial rites.

> When it was almost time for the Jewish Passover, Jesus went up to Jerusalem. In the Temple courts he found men selling cattle, sheep and doves, and other sitting at tables exchanging money. So he made a whip out of cords and drove all from the Temple area, both sheep and cattle; he scattered the coins of the money changers and overturned their tables. To those who sold doves he said, Get these out of here! How dare you turn my Father's house into a market? (John 2:13-16 NIV)

Because this is the only incident recorded in the Bible of Jesus taking direct action against the system, it makes a powerful statement regarding his opposition to sacrificial worship. But because Christian exegetes have paid little attention to the Old Testament condemnation of animal sacrifice—either ignoring or rationalizing it—they have lacked any sense of the profanity that its continuation represented to Jesus. Consequently, the theories they have offered for his uncharacteristic action have totally missed the mark.

The usual explanation is that Christ was angry because the money-changers were cheating the people. Alternatively, it is said that the preslaughter procedures at the Temple had become "too commercial." But there are no biblical or extra-biblical facts on which to base such theories. The Bible does not say that people were being cheated; and providing coins for the purchase of animals was a necessary part of the sacrificial system. From all accounts, Jesus was never overly concerned with the monetary practices of his time. [2] He even had a tax collector among his disciples at a time when these men were detested by the Jewish people.

In refusing to acknowledge the importance that Israel's prophets gave to the abolition of sacrifices, traditional Christianity has followed the footsteps of Orthodox Judaism. After the era of the Latter Prophets, the Hebrews rebuilt their altars and reinstituted animal sacrifice. And after the death of Jesus, Christianity reinstituted the value of sacrifice by claiming that the God who could not be appeased by the perpetual slaughter of animals was finally appeased by the sacrifice of His son. In both instances, the idea that slaughter is pleasing to God was reestablished. This allowed human beings to continue to project upon God their own appetite for vengeance and violence. Again and again, men have insisted on portraying God

---

2. Matt. 22:17–21.

as One who demanded the death of helpless creatures to appease his anger or to assuage his sense of "justice."

Yet the Scriptures continue to witness to a God whose nature precludes such violence. They tell of a Creator whose love and compassion extends to all creatures.

In the tradition of the Latter Prophets, Jesus described God as a loving parent, One who "causes his sun to rise on the evil and the good." Christ urged his followers to demonstrate the same goodness to all creatures—even to those whom they considered their enemies. The word "enemy" had too long been an excuse for murder and mayhem.

> You have heard it was said, Love your neighbor and hate your enemy. But I tell you Love your enemies and pray for those who persecute you that you may be the sons of your Father in Heaven. He causes his sun to rise on the evil and the good and sends rain on the righteous and the unrighteous. (Matt. 6:43–45 NIV)

Jesus described his own ministry as one of caring for others, and he often referred to animals to make this point. In so doing, he was testifying to the ability of nonhuman creatures to demonstrate characteristics of love and concern. In the gospel of Matthew, Christ likened his desire to protect and care for his people to the desire of a mother hen to care for her young:

> O, Jerusalem, Jerusalem . . . how often I have longed to gather your children together as a hen gathers her chicks under her wings, but you would not. (Matt. 23:37)

More often, Jesus used the behavior of lambs to make his point. He likened his own role to that of the care-giving shepherd. In John's gospel he refers to himself by a title that has remained through the ages: Jesus designated himself "The Good Shepherd." (John 10:14)

Just as the shepherds who were caring for their flocks around Bethlehem played an important part at the birth of Christ, so the relationship between shepherd and sheep played an important part in his adult life. Jesus frequently likened that relationship to his own calling. In so doing, he was continuing in the tradition of the prophet Isaiah, who had used the same idea to express God's loving care for all creation:

> Here is your God . . . . He tends his flock like a shepherd:
> He gathers the lambs in his arms and carries them close to
> his heart; he gently leads those that have young. (Isaiah
> 40:9, 11 NIV)

Jesus used these images as symbols of God's relatedness to human beings, but he was also reminding people that an ideal relationship with animals was one in which they were the object of man's concern and care. The life of the shepherd was a life of human service to nonhuman creatures. It was a lifestyle that Jesus consistently held up as a model to his followers.

Despite God's having ordained men to care for animals, and despite the prophets' denunciations of sacrificial worship, the slaughter had continued. In biblical times, lambs were most frequently sacrificed. Their gentleness made them the ideal victims. Neither priest nor penitant had to deal with the frenzied—and dangerous—struggles of a creature faced with death. Consequently, sheep were endlessly slaughtered as atonements for sin, as thanksgiving offerings, and as redemptors for more valuable animals.

The nonviolent nature of the lamb being led to slaughter was also a basis for the designation of Jesus as "the Lamb of God." Like the lamb, Christ did not attempt to inflict violence on those who wanted to kill him. When the authorities came to arrest him in Gethsemene, he ordered his followers to refrain from retaliation. And when one of his disciples attacked and wounded a man, Jesus ordered him to sheath his weapon: "Put your sword back," he said, "for all who draw the sword will die by the sword." (Matt. 26:52)

Refusing to meet violence with violence, Jesus went to his death "like a sheep that is led to the slaughter-house." (Acts 8:32)

Years before it took place, John the Baptist had predicted Christ's manner of death. When Jesus first began his ministry, the Baptist had called out regarding him, "Behold the Lamb of God." (John 1:29) And after his death the disciples of Jesus continued to identify him with the animals he had so often referred to during his life. "The Good Shepherd" had forever become the "Lamb of God." Just as animals were sacrificed because men thought this was pleasing to God, so Jesus of Nazareth—said to be a blasphemer— was slain because men thought this would be pleasing to God.

THE BOOK
OF REVELATION:
THE LIFE TO COME

THE IDENTIFICATION OF CHRIST with the animal
kingdom is continued in the Book of Revelation. That
book tells of things that are to come and is the record of
a vision given to John, a disciple of Jesus, a few decades
after the crucifixion. In that vision the "Lamb" has a
pivotal role. John's vision told of an afterlife—of
another kind of existence—wherein happiness would
be unmarred because "God shall wipe away all tears."
(Rev. 21:4)

For almost 2000 years countless women and men
have clung to a hope of the kind of afterlife recorded in
Revelation. They have held this hope for themselves
and for their loved ones.

John's revelation has continued to play a crucial role
in giving hope to human hearts. Although his vision
did not give an answer to "why" life holds so much
pain and misery, it did promise that such suffering
would end. The Book of Revelation promises that there
will be a new heaven and a new earth in which "there
shall be no more death, neither sorrow, nor crying,

neither shall there be anymore pain; for the former things are passed away." (Rev. 21:4)

Revelation also tells of a time when human beings will gather around the throne of God. There they will sing songs of praise and joy. And John's vision tells something more about that heavenly existence: It reveals that God's other creatures—the animals—will join in that heavenly chorus.[1]

John's prophetic vision of an afterlife that includes animals was a continuation—and a completion—of the message given by the Latter Prophets. Those men had begun the task of bringing to consciousness the fact that nonhuman creatures were of great value in God's sight: The prophets foretold a world in which animals, as well as humans, would exist in peace and contentment. These prophets taught that when human beings had ceased their violence, the violence of animals would also be a thing of the past. Then, together, animals and humans would enjoy the blessed existence of a restored creation: The lion and the lamb will lie down together and a little child will lead them. (Isa. 11:6)

But although the scriptures repeatedly witness to the high value that the Creator places on animal life, human beings have been reluctant to accept that truth. They have been aided and abetted in that reluctance by biblical scholars. Prompted by human chauvinism, many scholars have gone to great lengths to obfuscate

1. Chapters 4 and 5, Book of Revelation.

the scriptural message of animal worth and animal afterlife. To do this, they have misused the tools of exegisis, symbolism, and translation. Nowhere is this misuse more apparent than in the book of Revelation.

Although Revelation is replete with signs and symbols, it also deals with eternal realities. And the existence of so many symbolic passages has never caused men to doubt the book's promise of their own redemption and restoration. When John's vision describes men enjoying the presence of the Creator in heavenly places, no scholars find this scenario unreasonable; neither do they consider this too high an honor for human beings. But when the same passages of scripture tell of the presence of animals in the same high places, scholars decided that the Bible really couldn't mean what it said: Surely animals are not worthy of such honor.

The first official refusal to believe what the scriptures said came about a hundred years after John's vision had been recorded. At that time, Iraneous, the bishop of Lyons, decided that passages telling of animals present in heaven didn't really mean what they said. He speculated, instead, that the four animals Revelation described as being gathered around the throne of God, couldn't really be symbols of animal creation. The bishop decided they were actually men—in disguise. He also decided that these men-disguised-as-animals were specific persons: namely, Matthew, Mark, Luke, and John, the Four Evangelists.

The biblical passages on which he based his conclusions are quoted below. They provide testimony to the bishop's original thinking rather than to his scriptural fidelity.

> Then, in my vision, I saw a door open in heaven and heard the same voice speaking to me .... Come up here: I will show you what is to come in the future. With that, the Spirit possessed me and I saw a throne standing in heaven, and the One who was sitting on the throne .... Around the throne in a circle ... I saw twenty-four elders sitting .... In the center, grouped around the throne itself, were four animals with many eyes, in front and behind. The first animal was like a lion, the second like a bull, the third animal had a human face, and the fourth animal was like a flying eagle.... Every time the animals glorified and honored and gave thanks to the One sitting on the throne, who lives for ever and ever, the twenty-four elders prostrated themselves before him to worship the One who lives for ever and ever .... (Rev. 4:1, 2, 4, 6, 7, 9, 10 JB)

Despite the chauvinism that prompted Iraneous and his successors to reject the scriptural references to animals in heaven, there are scholarly works that give accurate information. These works note that the four animals described in Revelation 4:7 are representative of nonhuman as well as human creatures. They also note that when the Bible describes these animals as having, repectively, the likenesses of a lion, an ox, an eagle, and a man, it is recording the fact that all kinds of God's creatures are represented in heaven. The four creatures "are the heads of animate creation; the lion of wild beasts, the ox of tame beasts, the eagle of birds; the man of all (mankind)." [2]

---

2. E.W. Bullinger, *A Critical Lexicon and Concordance to the English and Greek New Testament* (Grand Rapids: Zondervan, 1975), p. 147.

There are other reference works that preserve the real meaning of these biblical verses that refer to animals. Unfortunately, they are not generally accessible. But they are accessible to exegetes and translators. Still, these scholars have continued to obscure the Bible's message of animal restoration. And in the twentieth century, it is the translators who have been most successful in confusing the issue.

In this century, there has been a proliferation of Bible translations. But until recently, the King James version—published in 1611—was the standard Bible for Protestant readers. And, too often, the archaic English of that translation served to confuse rather than clarify the Greek text. This is what happened in the matter of biblical references to animals.

The King James Bible never uses the term *animal*. As far as it is concerned, the word might as well not exist. Instead it uses the word *beast*. And it is used whether the meaning implied is positive, neutral, or pejorative. Consequently, the positive message of Revelation 4:7 that refers to the "four beasts" gathered around the throne of God is juxtaposed to the very negative use of the word when it refers to the dreaded Beast of the Apocalypse: the Beast that wars on God's people.

But although the King James translation did not distinguish between "beast" and "animal," the Greek language does. And Greek is the language in which the New Testament is written. Modern English makes the same distinction. *Zoon* is the Greek equivalent of the word *animal* and it is used to refer to nonhuman creatures in general. *Therion* is equivalent to the word *beast* and has the same English connotation of a savage and brutish creature.

This equivalent usage of English and Greek would seem to insure the accurate translation of passages referring to animals. But the use of modern English cannot overcome another obstacle that stands in the way of accurate translation: Too often, the bias of a translator can subtly, or grossly, distort the meaning of a text. This has been especially true of the verses in Revelation that depict animals, as well as humans and angels, enjoying the presence of their Creator.

As long as the archaic language of the King James Bible allowed scholars to read that "beasts" were admitted into the presence of God, it was relatively easy to decide—as Bishop Iraneous had done—that the scriptures did not really mean what they said. Translators could reason that savage and brutish creatures would hardly be singing God's praises in heavenly places. But this human chauvinism was somewhat shaken when modern scholars were faced with the fact that *zoon* is correctly translated as *animal*—not as *beast*. When the proper translation is made, the negative connotation that the word *beast* has for the modern reader is no longer present.

Because *animal* is a neutral, general term, its use in translation would have made it difficult for scholars to keep insisting that the Bible is referring to four men in disguise when it plainly says four animals.

Several other passages in the book of Revelation posed a similar threat to human prejudice. Some of those passages mention three different kinds of God's creatures—human, angel, and animal—in the same sentence. This kind of verse made it even harder to maintain that the animals mentioned were merely symbolic references to men.

> Every time the animals glorified and honored and gave thanks to the One sitting on the throne, who lives for ever and ever, the twenty-four elders prostrated themselves before Him to worship the One . . . . (Rev. 4:9 JB)

> And all the angels who were standing in a circle around the throne surrounding the elders and the four animals, prostrated themselves before the throne worshiping God. (Rev. 7:11 JB)

Scripture verses like these challenged the prejudices of some scholars. But they were able to meet the challenge. They did so by totally disregarding the intent of scripture. They opted for a legalistic translation that was as misleading as it was dishonest. The word *zoon*—the word that means *animal* in the Greek text—was not translated as animal. Instead, it was translated as *living creature*. This translation had a two-fold advantage: It was nebulous enough to obscure the biblical message concerning animals, and the definition was "legal."

It was legal because modern American dictionaries define *animal* as anything that is not a plant or as any living organism. But such definitions are general and are inadequate for particular situations. No one trying to communicate a message regarding animals would use the term *living creatures*; to do so would only cause confusion. A sign that said NO LIVING CREATURES

ALLOWED would be more confusing than informative. It could be forbidding the entrance of bird, beast, or human being. In the same way, when they translated the scriptures to read that "living creatures" are grouped around the throne of God, scholars confused the issue and obscured the Bible's specific reference to animals.

Translators were aware of the confusion that their terminology caused, so they took care to ensure that they did not translate *zoon* as *living creature* when such confusion served no purpose. The following verses illustrate this point.

> But these men revile the things they do not understand ... like unreasoning *animals*. (Jude 1:10 NAS)

> For the bodies of those *animals* whose blood is brought into the holy place by the high priest as an offering for sin are burned outside the camp. (Heb. 13:11 NAS)

In each of the above verses, the word *zoon* is correctly translated as *animal*. And it is translated this way by the same scholars who substitute the words *living creatures* when they are translating the Book of Revelation.

This scholarly prejudice against translating the Greek text accurately when it says that animals share in an afterlife colored the translation of most modern versions of the Bible. But there is a notable exception: The Jerusalem Bible correctly translates *zoon* as animal—even in the book of Revelation.

The men who produced this version of the Bible were able to maintain fidelity to the Greek text because their belief system was not threatened by a correct translation. The Jerusalem Bible was produced by Catholic scholars; and their religious tradition long ago settled questions about who or what went to heaven. By contrast, the diversity of Protestant beliefs does not permit a definite repository of doctrine—a *magisterium*—to bolster beliefs. Consequently, when faced with scriptural verses that pictured a human/animal togetherness in heavenly places, Protestant scholars protected their prejudice and their sensibilities. Catholic scholars were already protected against such ideas.

But it is an encouraging sign of the times in Western civilization that such prejudices need protection. Until a century ago, human consciousness had not developed to the point where animal welfare was a matter of wide concern. It was only after the obscenities of slavery and war—often justified by biblical theologians—were seriously questioned that an insight into the evils of animal exploitation began.

EPILOGUE:
THE SIGNS OF THE TIMES

"... can ye not discern the signs of the times?" (Matt. 16:3)

THEOLOGIANS OF VARIOUS persuasions discuss the necessity of understanding what the "signs of the times" are saying. By this they mean the ability to relate the various developments that are taking place in the world to the ongoing revelation of God. Properly discerned, these signs can tell us where the Spirit of God is leading.

In the past, practical consideration of basic human needs kept most people from responding to the fact that the treatment of animals is often unnecessarily cruel and exploitative. The need for animal skins for bodily protection long co-existed with the belief that adequate nutrition meant the eating of flesh. And the need for animals to do the work of farming, building, and commerce often resulted in their abuse. But in our own day, various scientific and technological developments have become "signs of the times": They have removed obstacles that once seemed to stand in the way of the humane treatment of animals. These developments have provided vastly superior alterna-

67

tives to the use and abuse of animals.

Many countries now have synthetic fabrics available to them. These materials provide more warmth and protection than animal fur. Lightweight and durable, synthetic products have eliminated the need to hunt, trap, and raise animals for their fur.

The introduction of "horseless carriages" began the widespread development of machinery that farmed, built, and transported the products of commerce more effectively than any work animal could do. This mechanization of labor effectively removed a main cause of animal abuse.

Barely a decade ago, mainstream nutritionists insisted that animal protein was of paramount importance in maintaining optimum health. This claim was bolstered by the constant dissemination of "evidence" that depicted the physiology of human beings as a schematic for carnivorism. That schematic was a misrepresentation of the facts. Today we know that the physiology of human beings—from teeth through arteries to intestines—gives irrefutable evidence that the optimum diet for human beings is not meat. In fact, the ingestion of meat puts an enormous strain on the entire body. And though there is still the attempt to include meat in the diet by decreasing its intake and increasing the ingestion of vegetables and grains, that effort at co-existence is doomed to failure. It is becoming obvious to the health care community that it is not the addition of plant foods to the diet that works seeming miracles; it is the removal of flesh foods that increases people's physical well-being.

The science of nutrition, the mechanization of labor, and the availability of synthetic fabrics are all "signs of the times"; they give notice that the age of the unthinking abuse of animals is coming to an end. It is ending because new knowledge and technology have undermined the rationale for such exploitation.

At the same time that technology is providing alternatives to animal-based products, communications between human and nonhuman beings has dramatically increased. In the past, the ability of animals was conveniently underrated, and the affection, loyalty, and intelligence they demonstrated was ignored or mislabelled "instinctive." We know now that their capacity for feeling and for communication is much more extensive and sophisticated than was formerly acknowledged. Pet-companions, for example, are credited with making an important contribution to the physical, mental, and emotional health of their owners. These pets are able to form bonds of empathy and affection because there is an underlying similarity of needs between them and the people with whom they interact.

Animals have also become eyes for the blind and ears for the deaf—trusted companions whose love and service are irreplaceable. Some animals have shown themselves able and willing to operate sophisticated machines for their paralyzed human companions, making life bearable for those who otherwise might not be able to endure. Through the use of signs, animals have even demonstrated the ability to communicate with human beings in a human language.

But at the same time that awareness of the similarities between humans and nonhumans has come to the fore, the brutalization of animals has found new avenues of expression. In laboratories and on campuses all over the country, the most sensitive and intelligent animals are subjected to atrocities. Labelled "research" by those who perform them, torturous experiments are carried out even when alternative methods provide superior results and render experimentation on living animals obsolete.

The refusal of many researchers to utilize available, alternative methods in the laboratory is similar to the refusal of many people to use alternatives to animal products in order to meet their clothing and fashion needs. Even when synthetic fabrics are readily available, there are consumers who still demand the skin, fur, teeth, and tusks of other creatures as decorations for their own bodies or as statements of their affluence. Technology can provide humane alternatives to the exploitation of animals, but society dictates whether or not humane treatment becomes the standard.

The decision to live life with respect and concern for all creatures that inhabit the earth is, first of all, an individual choice. But if the human race is to evolve spiritually and morally, that choice must eventually reflect a societal standard. The Kingdom of God promised by the Bible is a kingdom in which humans and nonhumans must live in peace with their own kind and with all other species. It is the world promised by the prophets, in which "the wolf also shall dwell with the lamb ... and the calf and the young lion and the fatling together, and a little child shall lead them." (Isa. 11:6)

The Kingdom of God, come to earth, is a kingdom in which justice, compassion, and love for all creatures will be a reality. It is the kind of world Jesus told His followers to expect when He taught them to pray:

Our Father which art in heaven, Hallowed be Thy name. Thy Kingdom come. Thy will be done, as in heaven, so in earth. (Luke 11:2)

AMEN.

BIBLIOGRAPHY

Albright, W.F. *The Biblical Period from Abraham to Ezra*. New York: Harper & Row, 1963.

Baron, Sale W. *A Social and Religious History of the Jews*. New York: Columbia University Press, 1958.

Barton, George. *The Religion of Israel*. New York: The Macmillan Company, 1918.

Bernstein, Leon. *Flavius Josephus: His Time and His Critics*. New York: Liveright Corporation, 1938.

Bright, John. *A History of Israel*. 3rd ed. Philadelphia: Westminster Press, 1972.

Bruce, F.F. *Israel and the Nations*. Grand Rapids: Wm. B. Eerdmans, 1969.

Buber, Martin. *The Prophetic Faith*. New York: Harper & Row, 1960.

Davidson, A.B. *The Theology of the Old Testament*. Edinburgh: T. & T. Clark, 1949.

de Vaux, Roland. *The Early History of Israel: To the Period of the Judges*. Philadelphia: Westminster Press, 1976.

Finkelstein, Louis. *The Pharisees: The Sociological Background of Their Faith*. 2 vols. Philadelphia: The Jewish Publication Society of America, 1946.

Foerster, Werner. *From the Exile to Christ: A Historical Introduction to Palestinian Judaism*. Philadelphia: Fortress Press, 1964.

Graetz, H. *History of the Jews*. Philadelphia: The Jewish Publishing Society of America, 1893.

Heschel, Abraham J. *The Prophets*. New York: Harper & Row, 1963.

Jeremias, Joachim. *Jerusalem in the Time of Jesus*. Philadelphia: Fortress Press, 1969.

Kadushin, Max. *The Rabbinic Mind*. New York: The Jewish Theological Seminary of America, 1952.

Kaufmann, Yehezkel. *The Religion of Israel: From Its Beginnings to the Babylonian Exile*. Chicago: University of Chicago Press, 1960.

Kohler, Kaufmann. *Jewish Theology*. New York: The Macmillan Company, 1932.

Manson, T.W. *The Teaching of Jesus: Studies in Form and Content*. Cambridge: At the University Press, 1955.

Noth, Martin. *The History of Israel*. New York: Harper & Brothers, 1960.

Reicke, Bo. *The New Testament Era: The World of the Bible From 500 B.C. to A.D. 100*. Philadelphia: Fortress Press, 1968.

Weber, Max. *Ancient Judaism*. New York: The Free Press, 1952.

Wright, Ernest F. *The Challenge of Israel's Faith*. Chicago: The University of Chicago Press, 1944.